Color Test Book

J and I Publishing

How to use this book

Whether you are a professional artist or not, you want to know that the color you are using is really what you want to reflect in your artwork. Often, colors look different on paper than they do on the cap or barrel of the product. This simple book offers you a place to test your colors and write down the numbers the manufacturer provides on colored pencils, markers and other art supplies.

On each page, you will find a simple design, repeated large enough that you can fill it in with color and write the number inside or below it. This way, you can keep a record of what all your colors look like and refer back to this book when you want to look at them before coloring.

In the last section of this book there is a place to take notes on brands of art supplies and an area to list the colors you need to reorder. As some markers and pens tend to bleed through and we have no control over the thickness of the paper in this book, we have also included a page at the front for you to cut out and put behind your color test pages to protect the other sheets.

Have fun exploring your world of color!

Cut out this page and insert behind the page you are currently coloring.

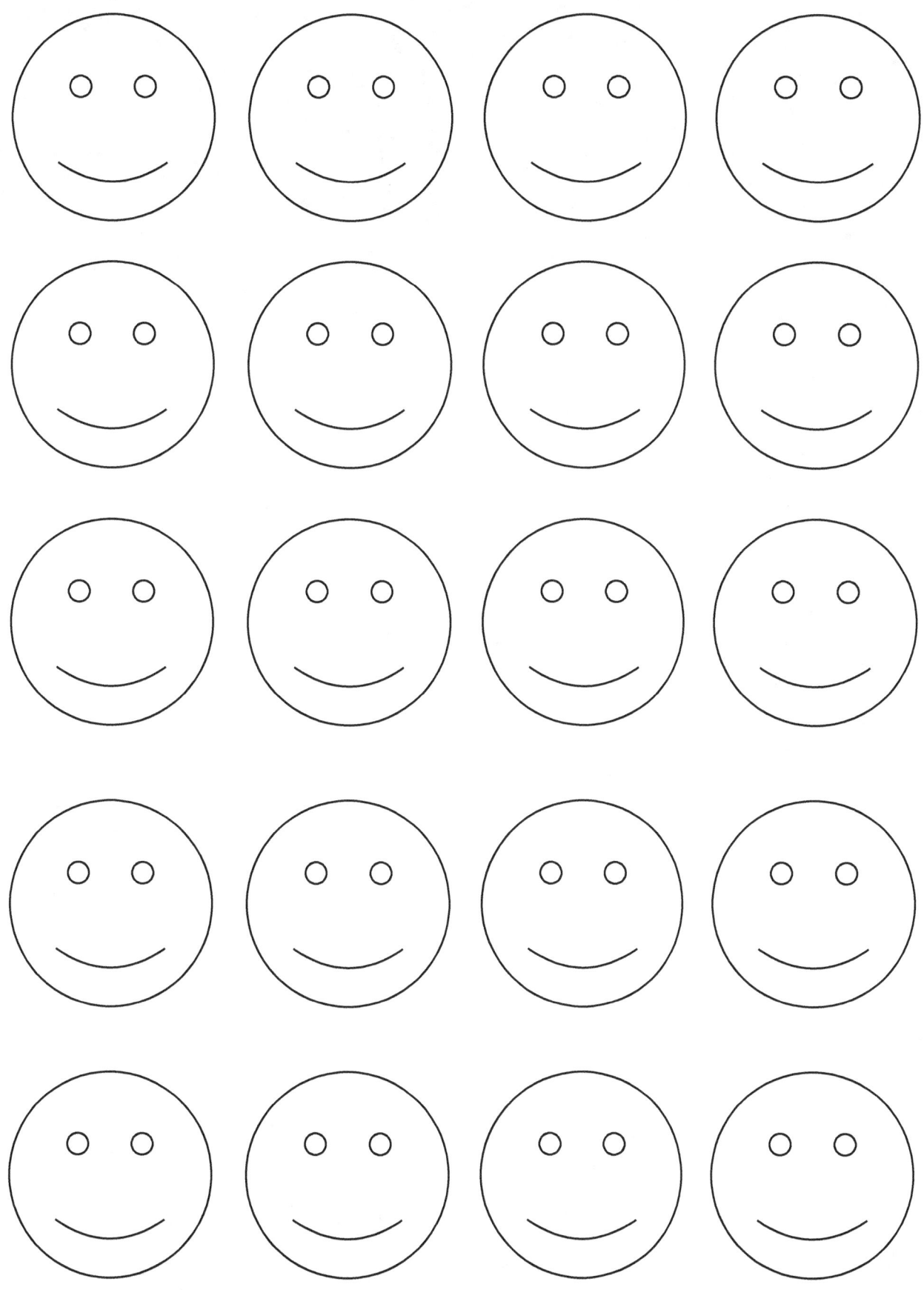

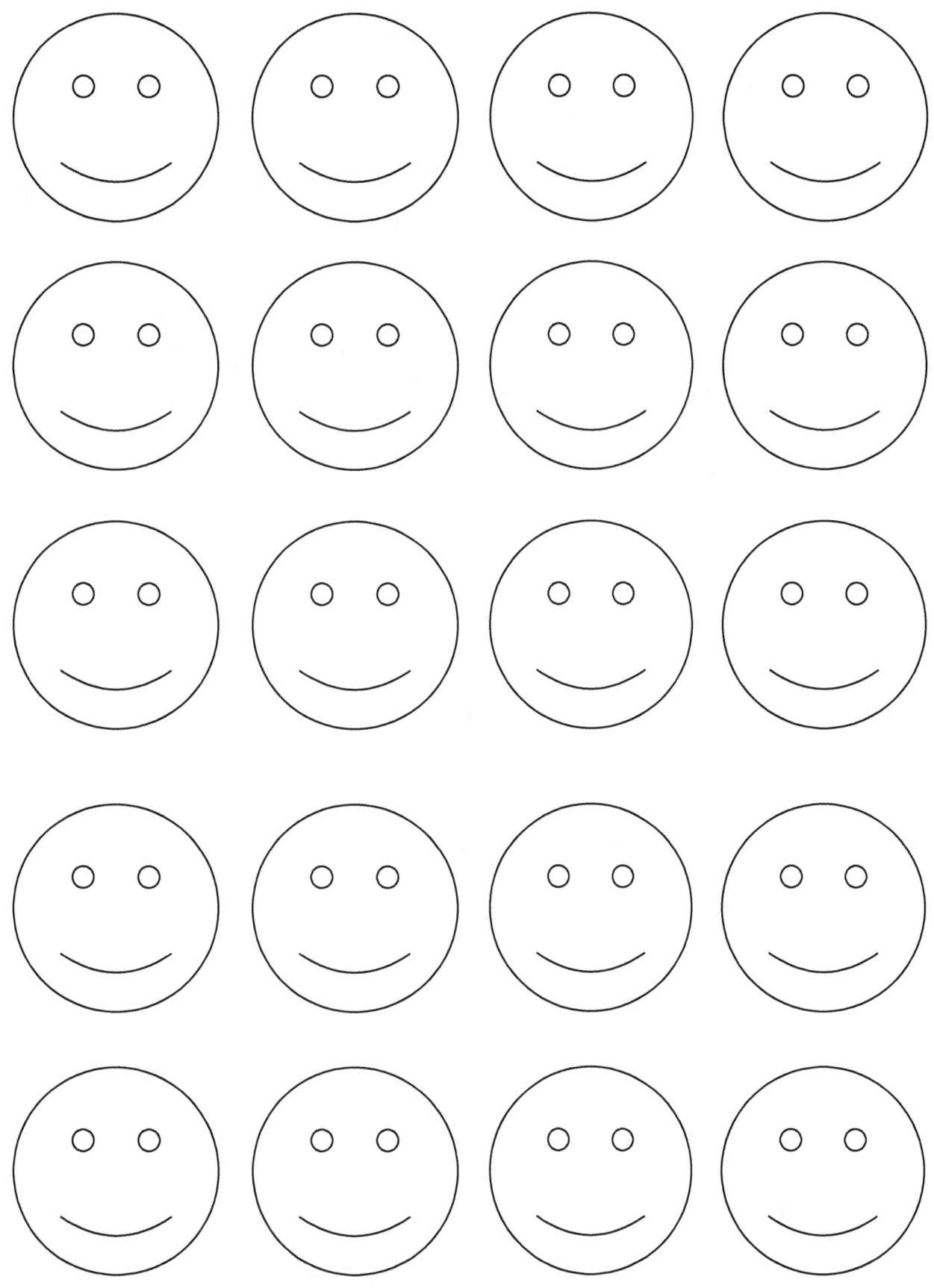

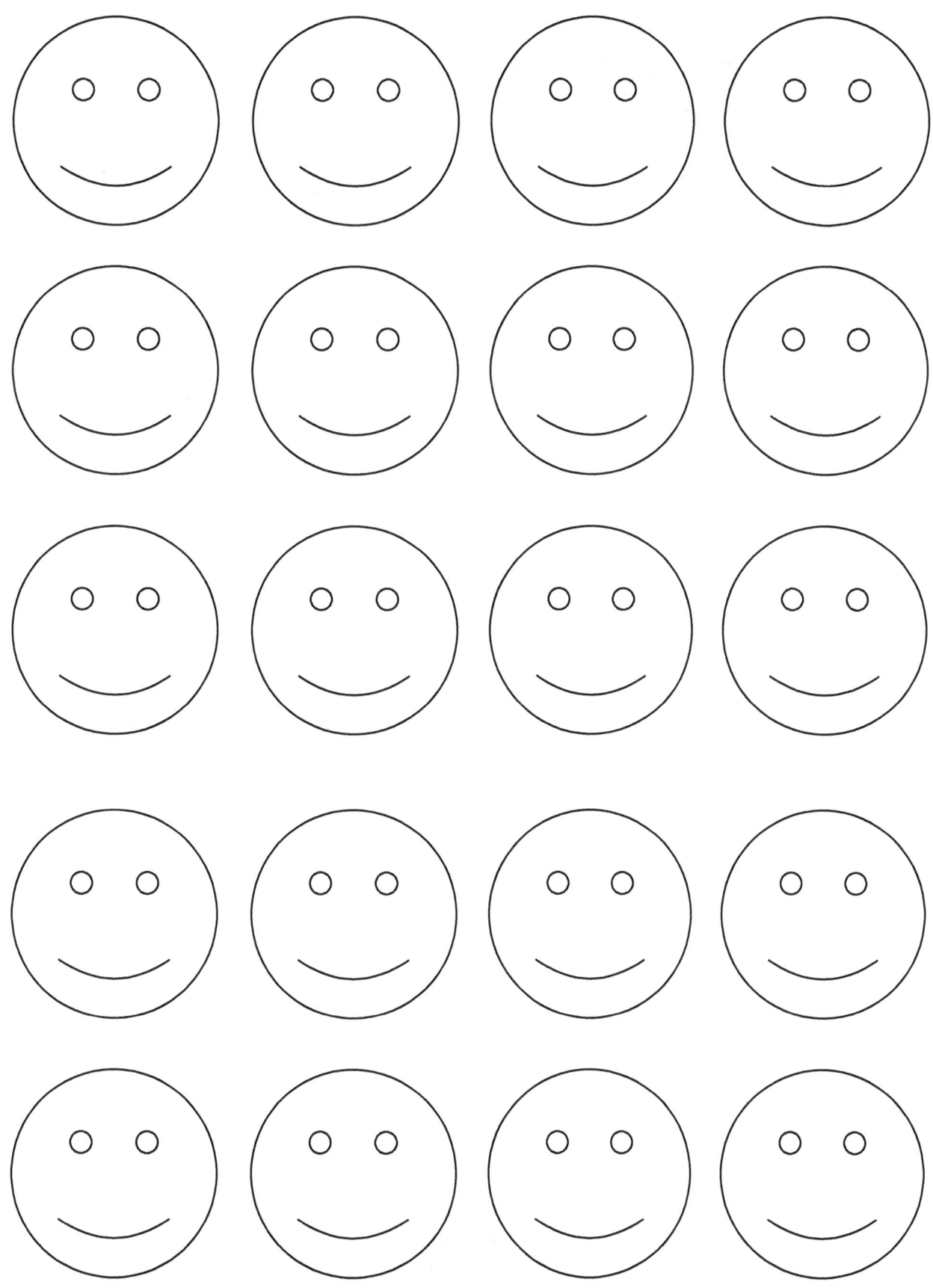

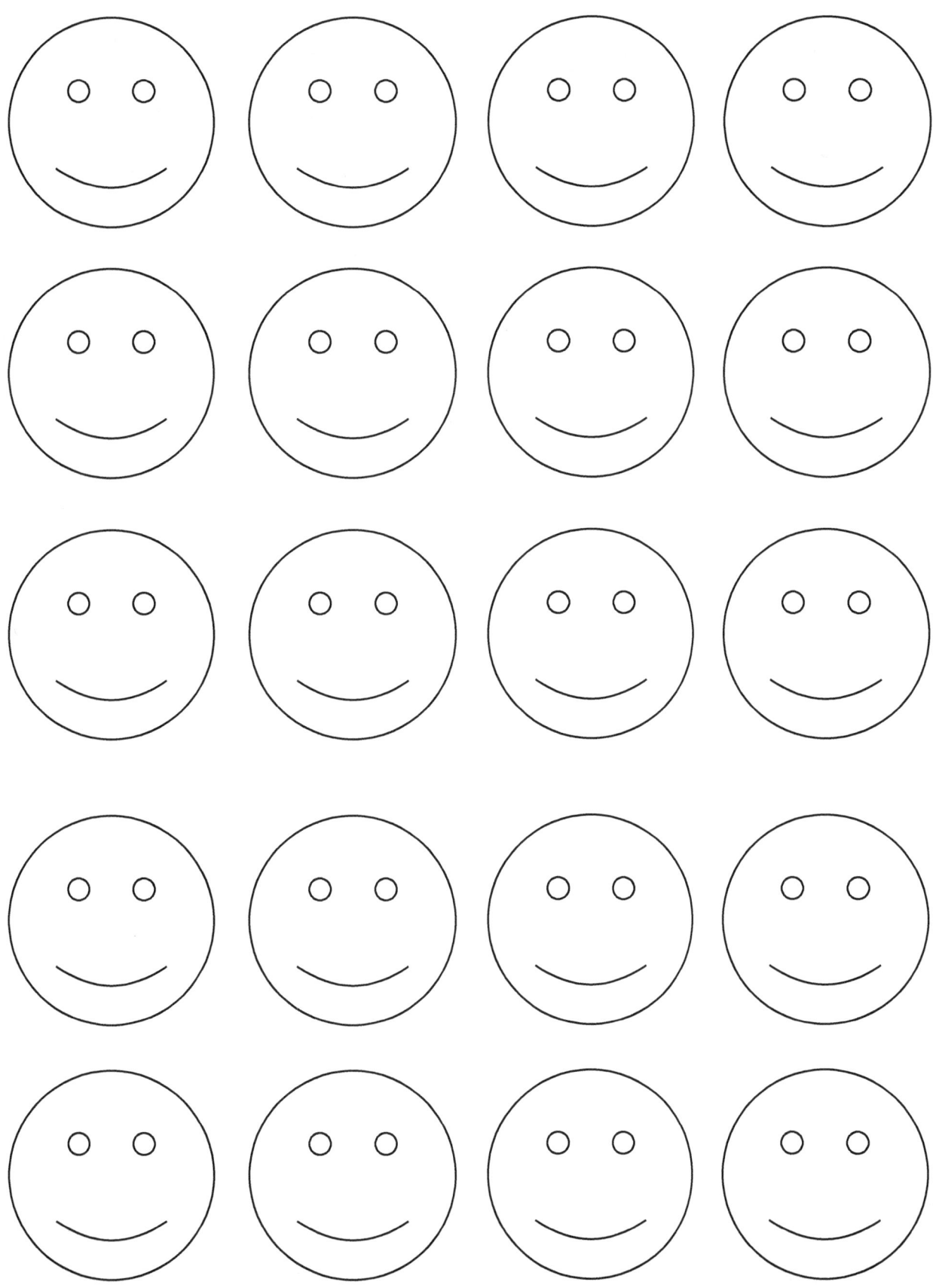

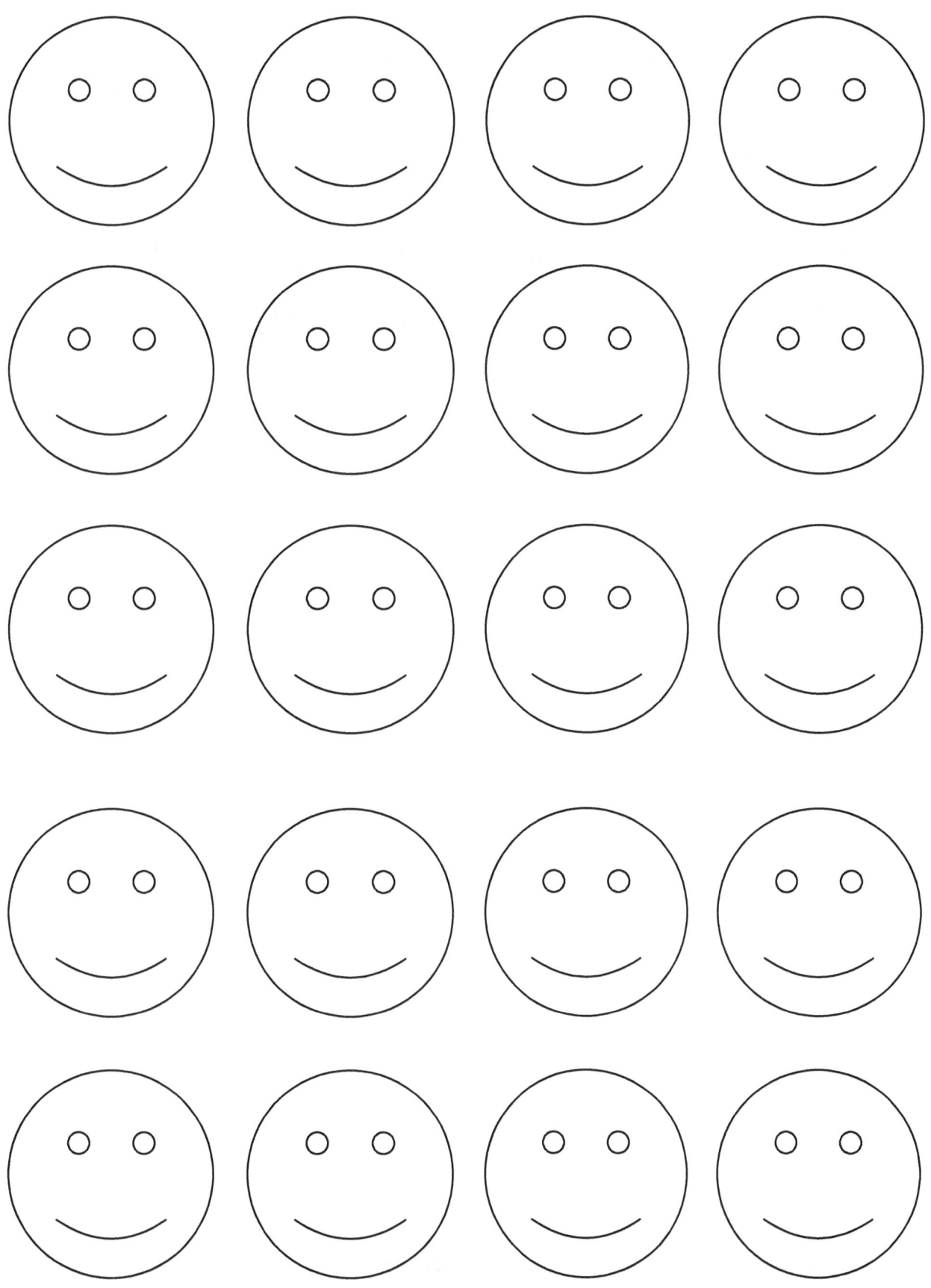

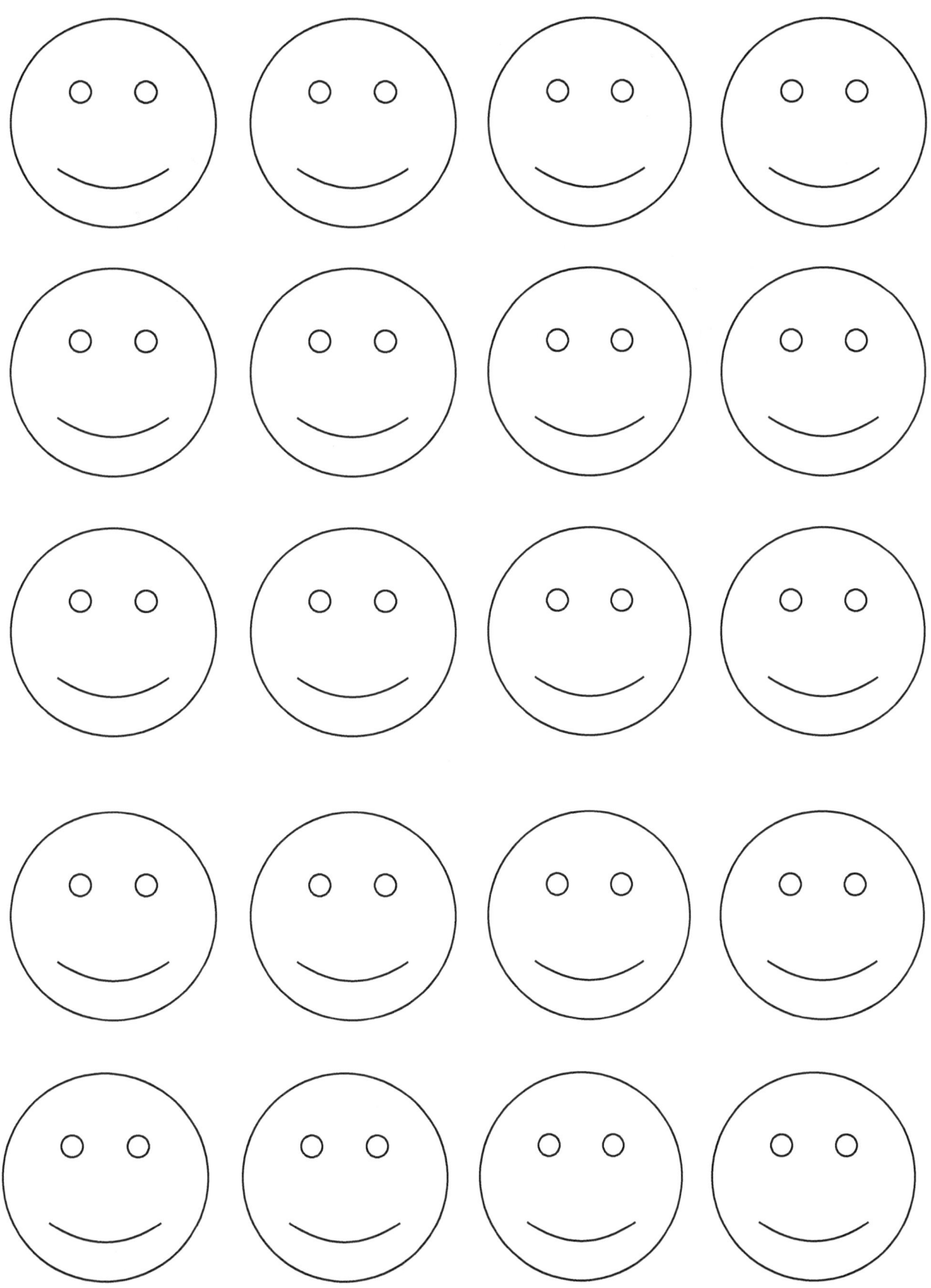

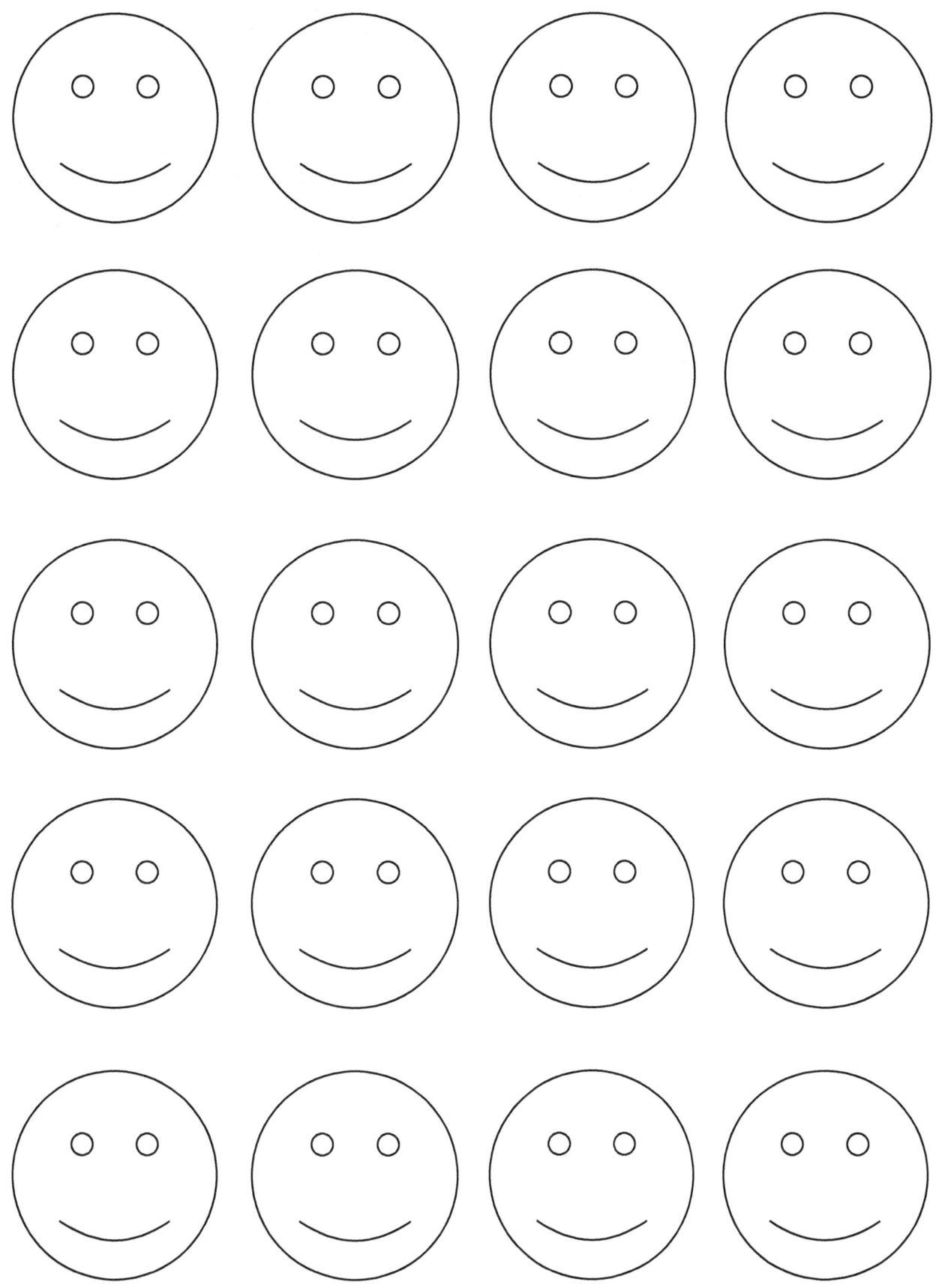

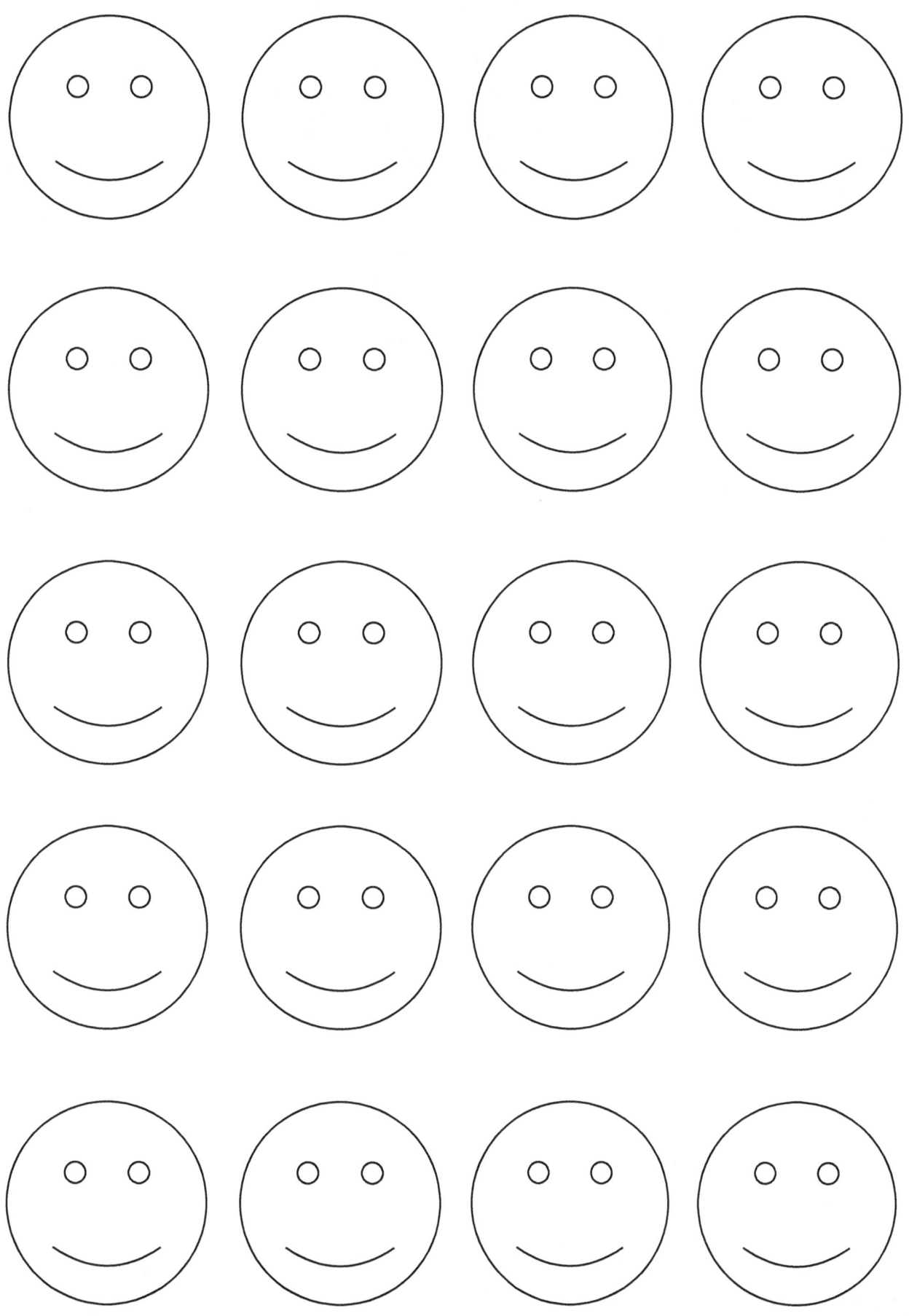

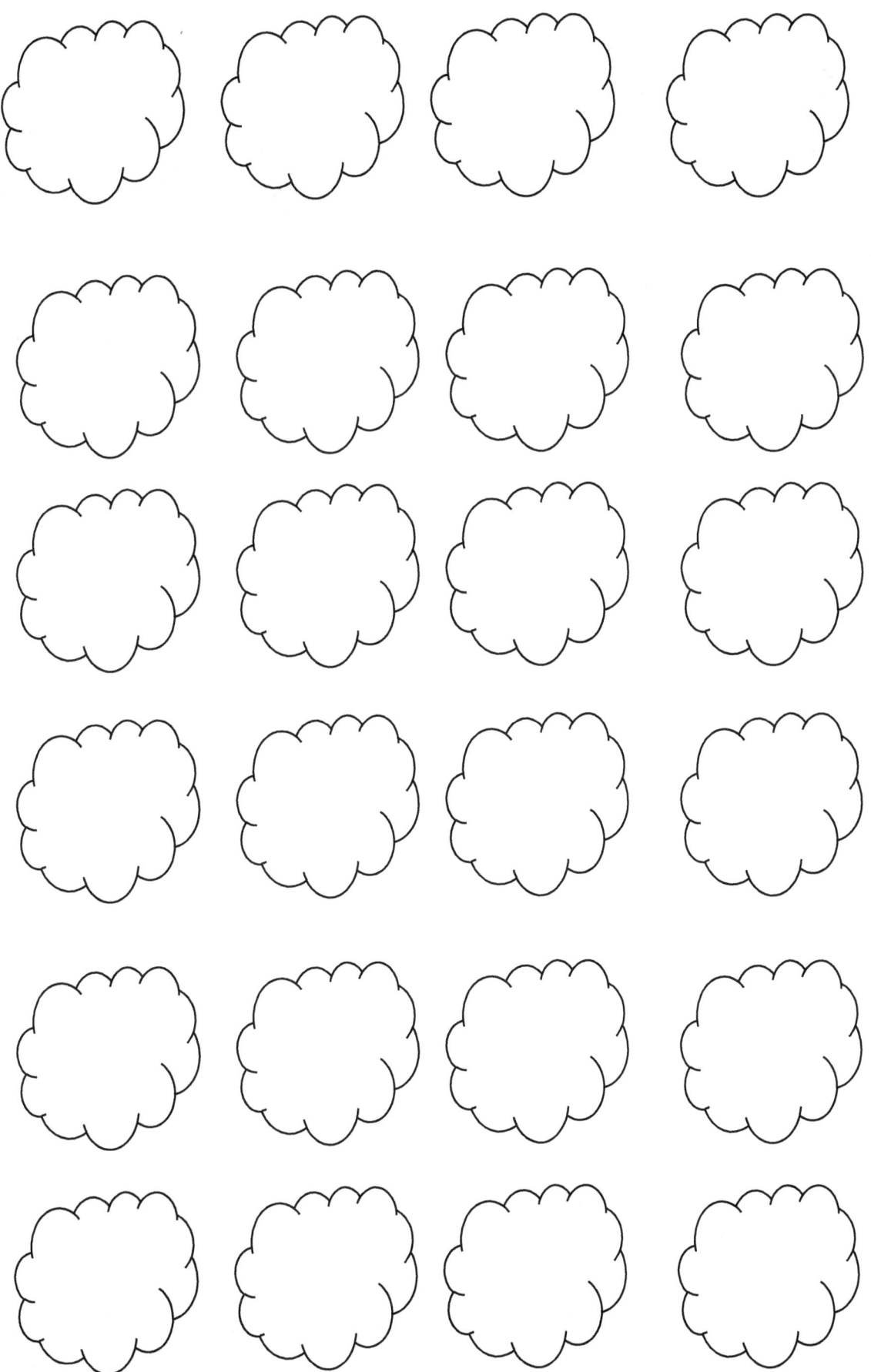

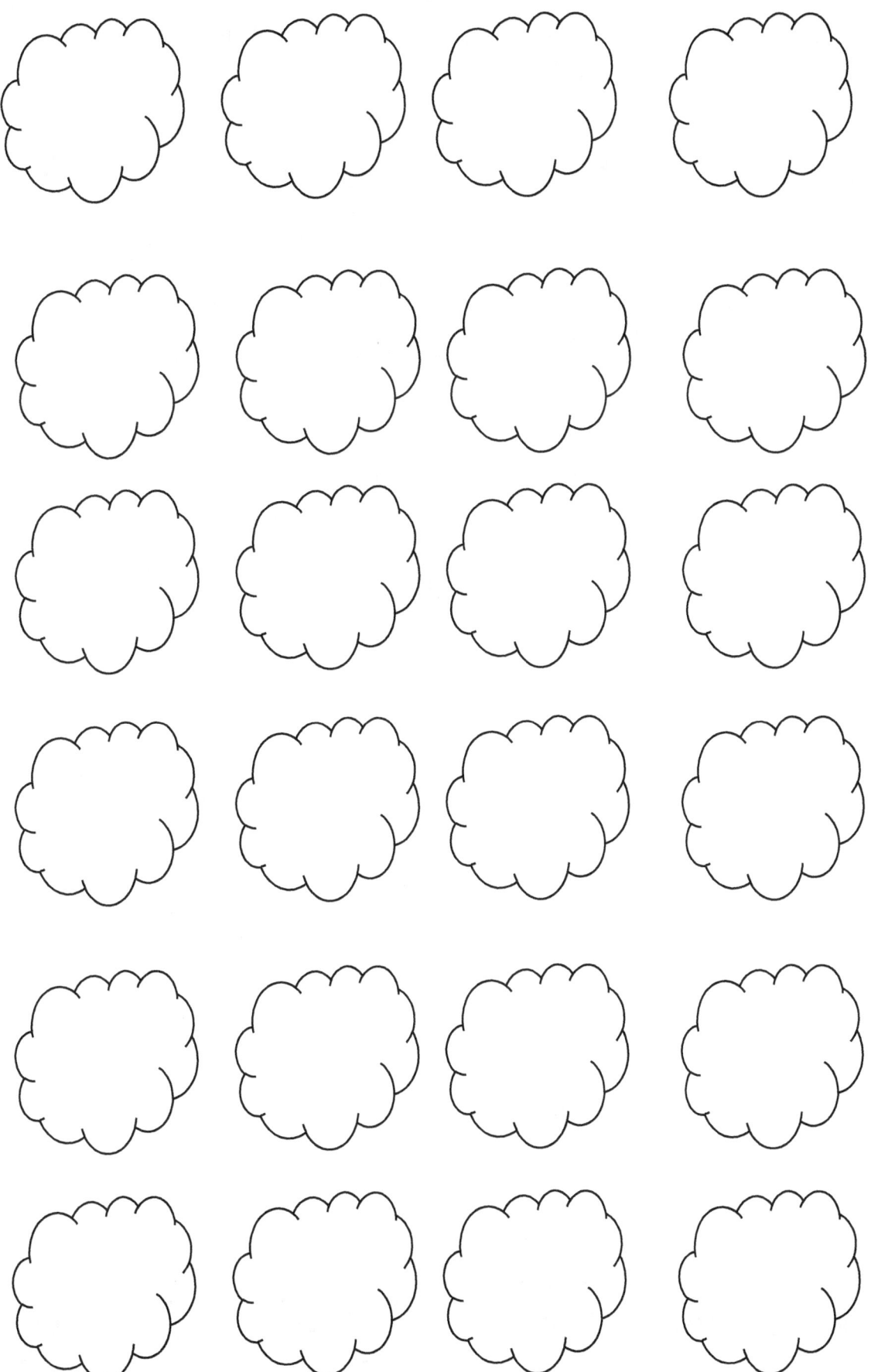

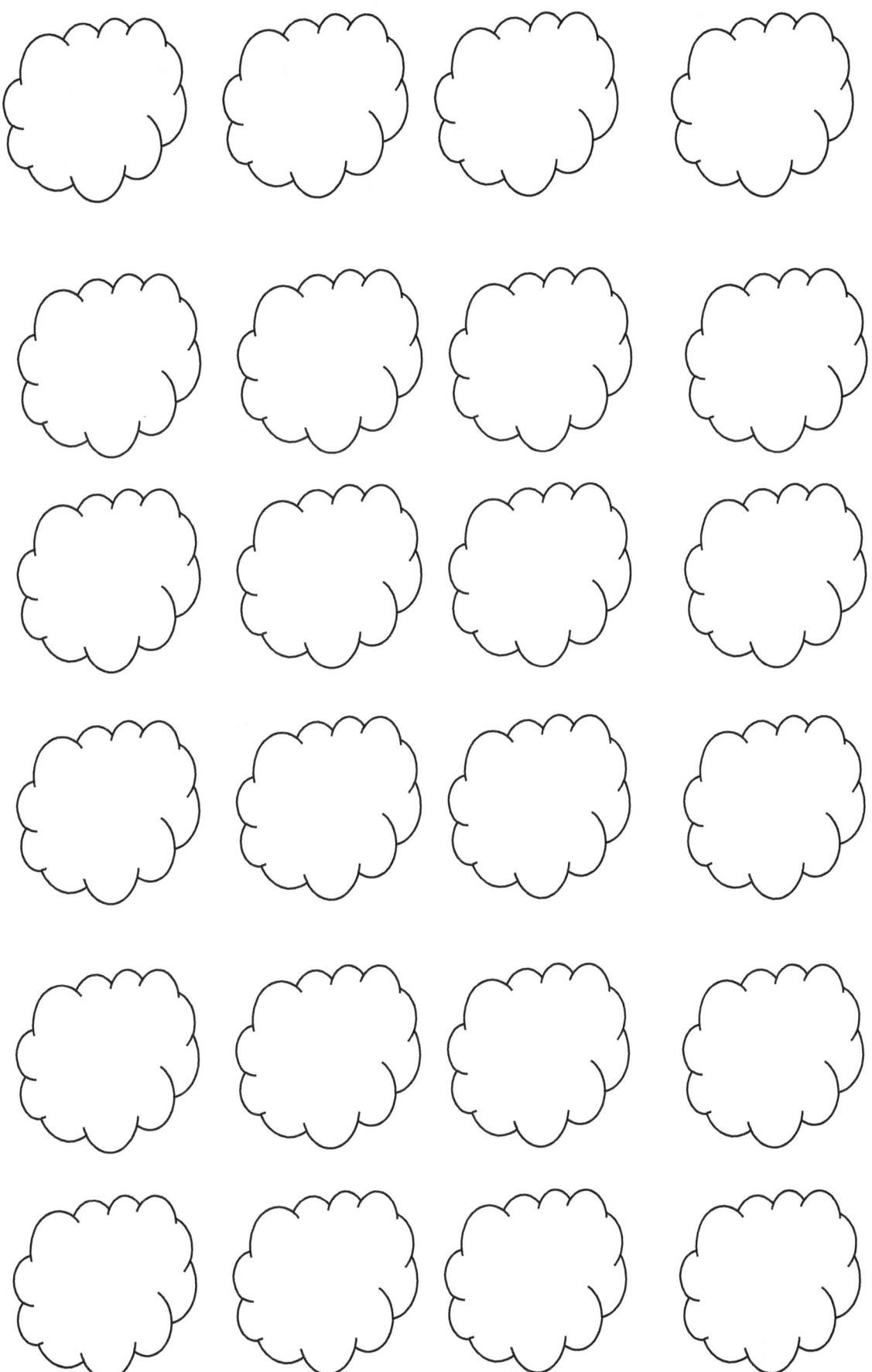

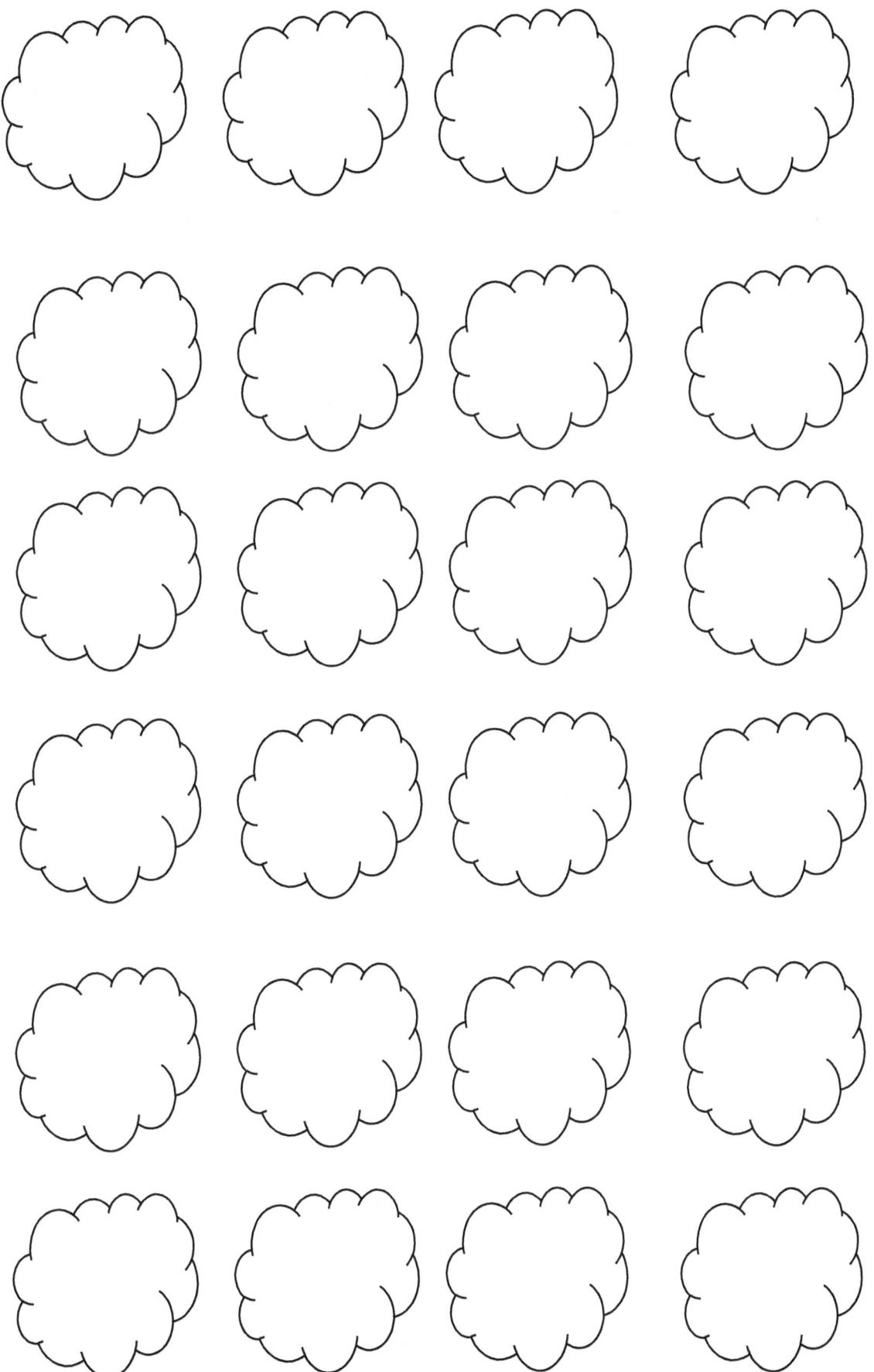

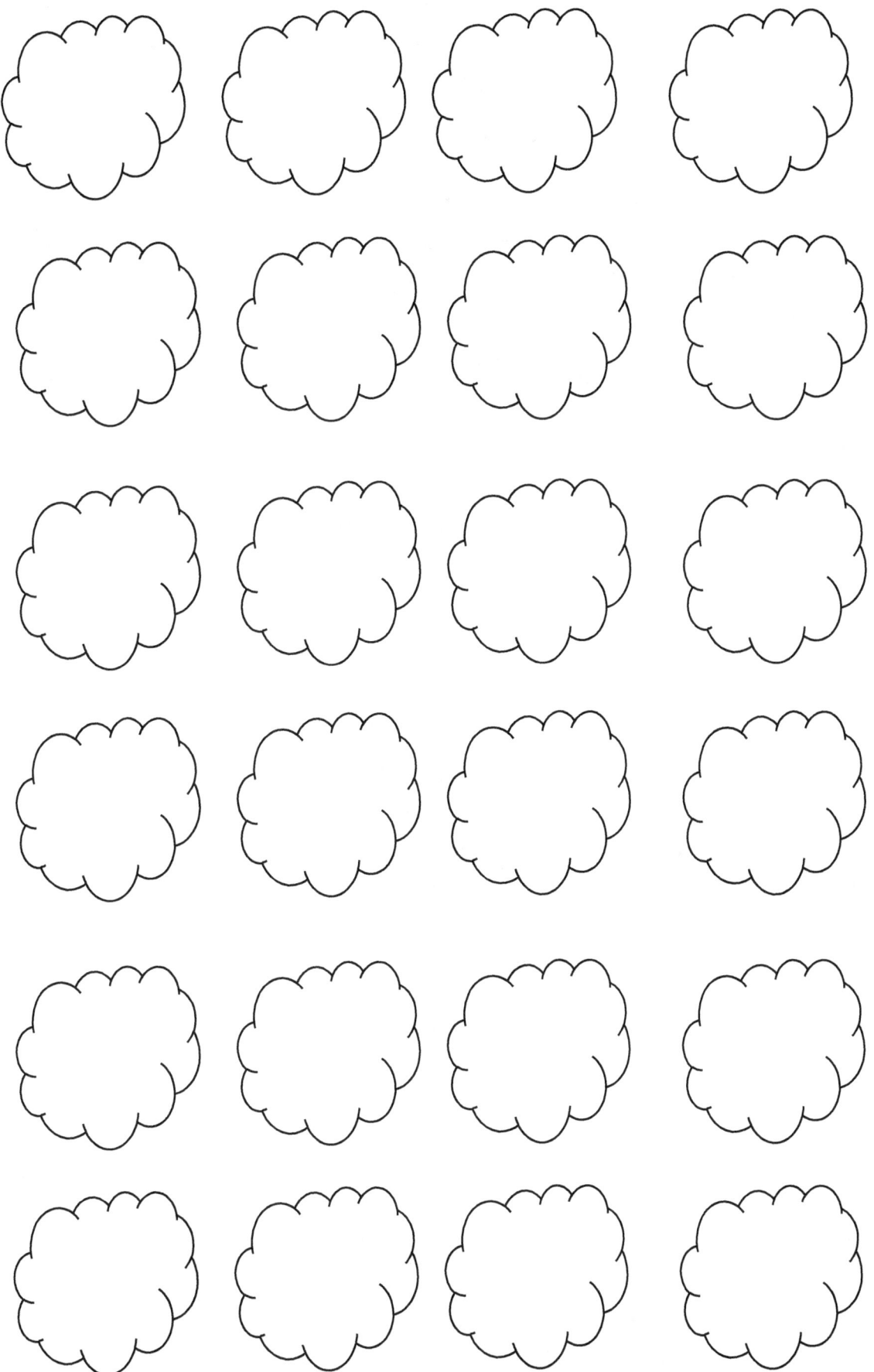

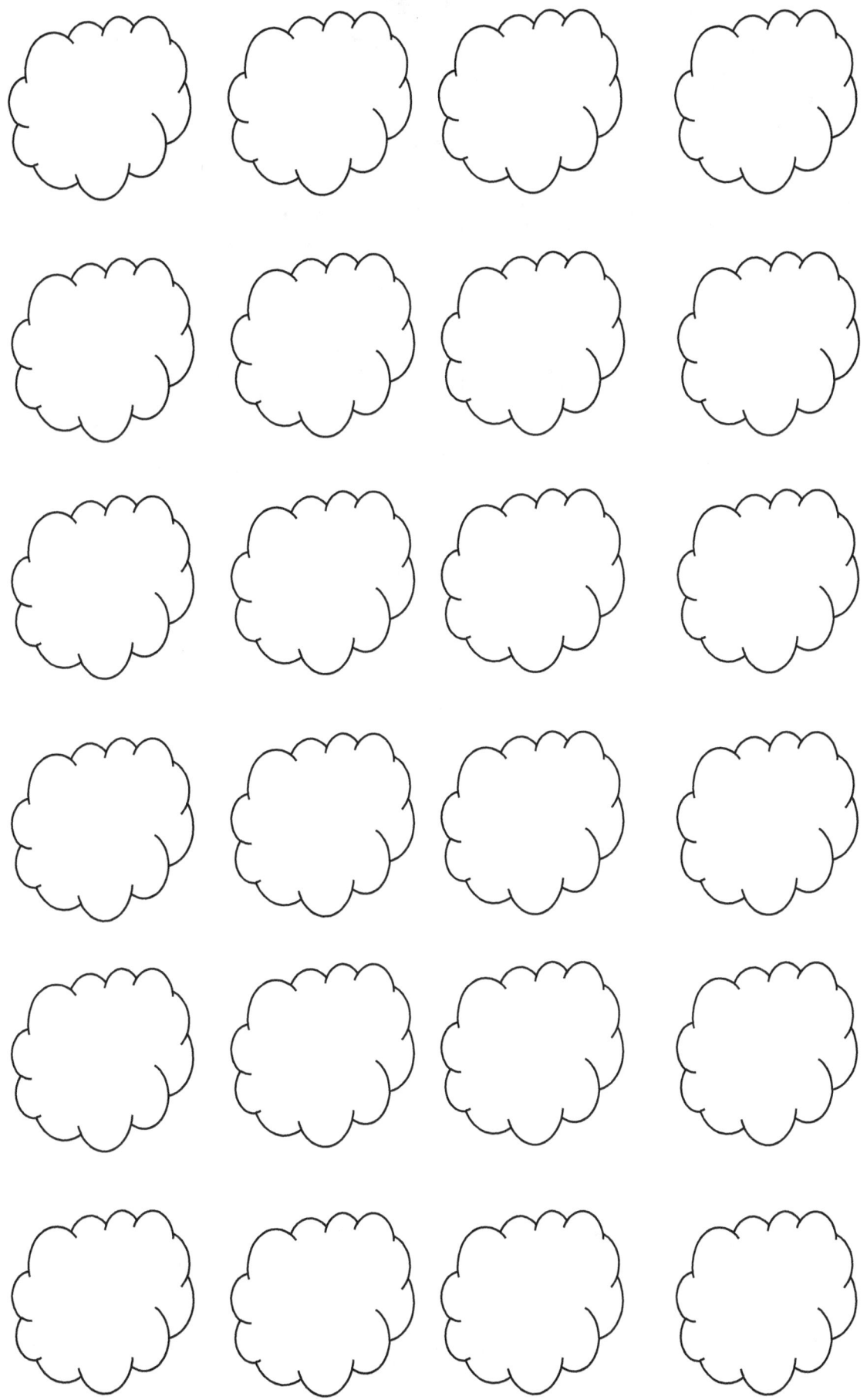

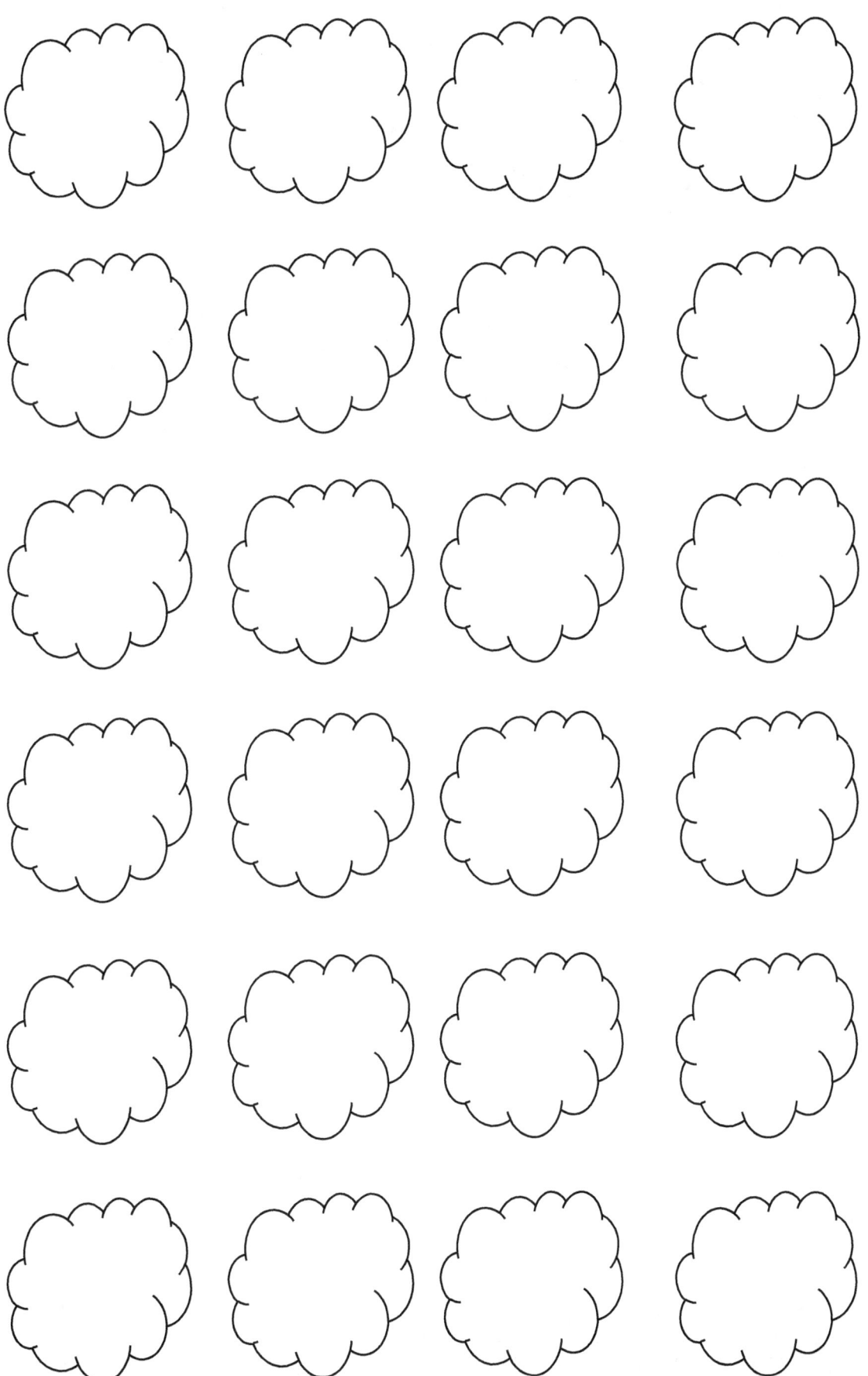

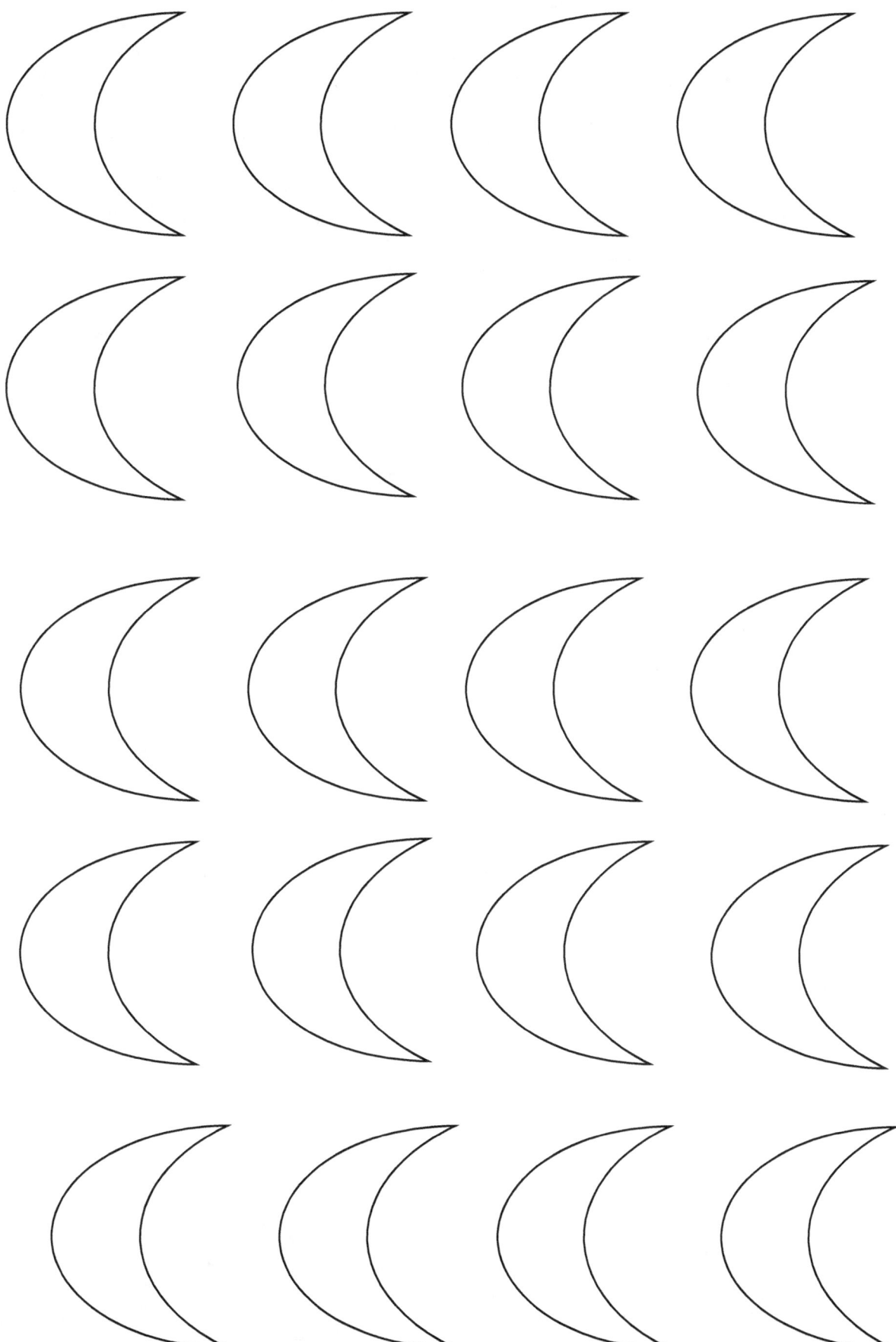

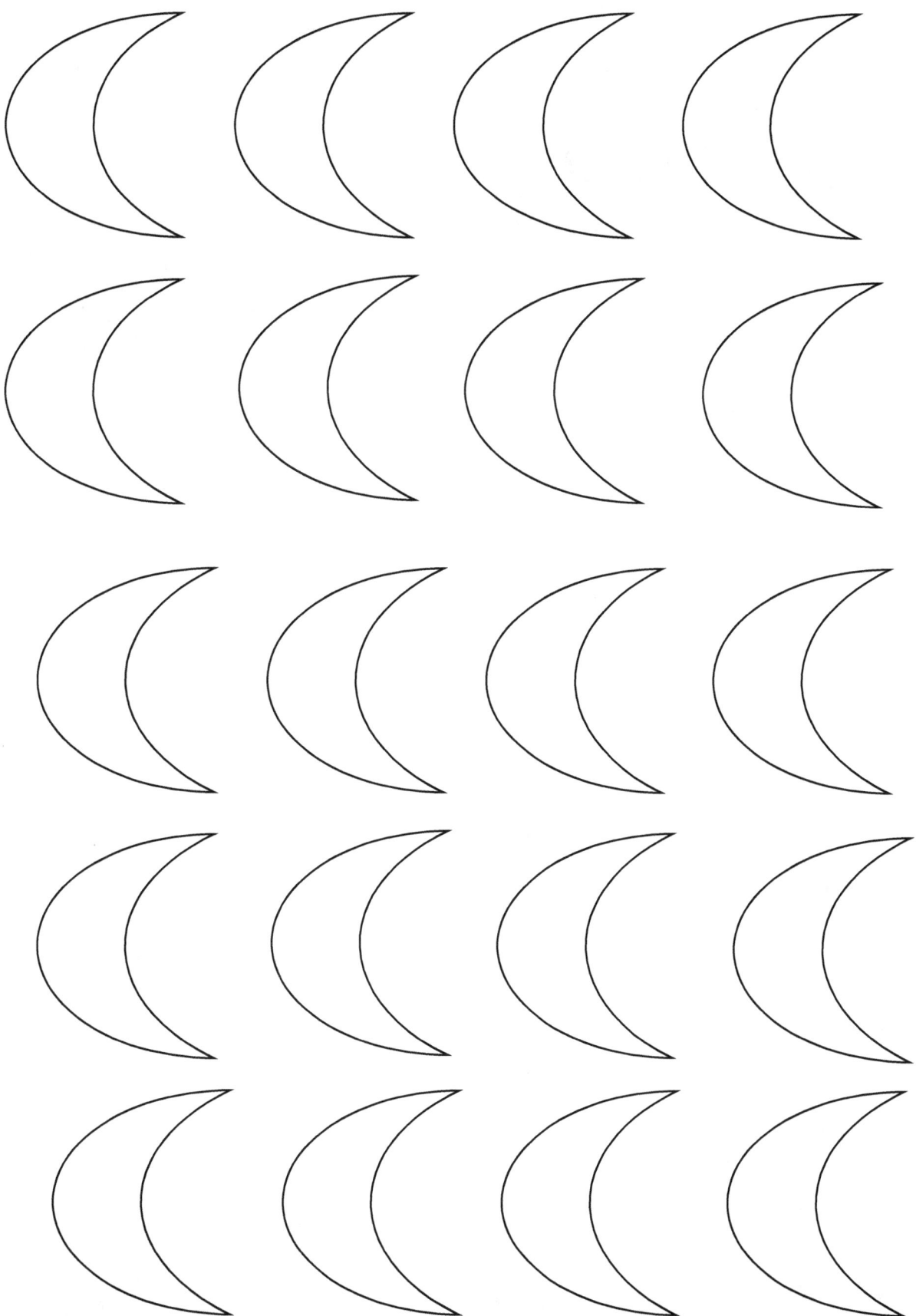

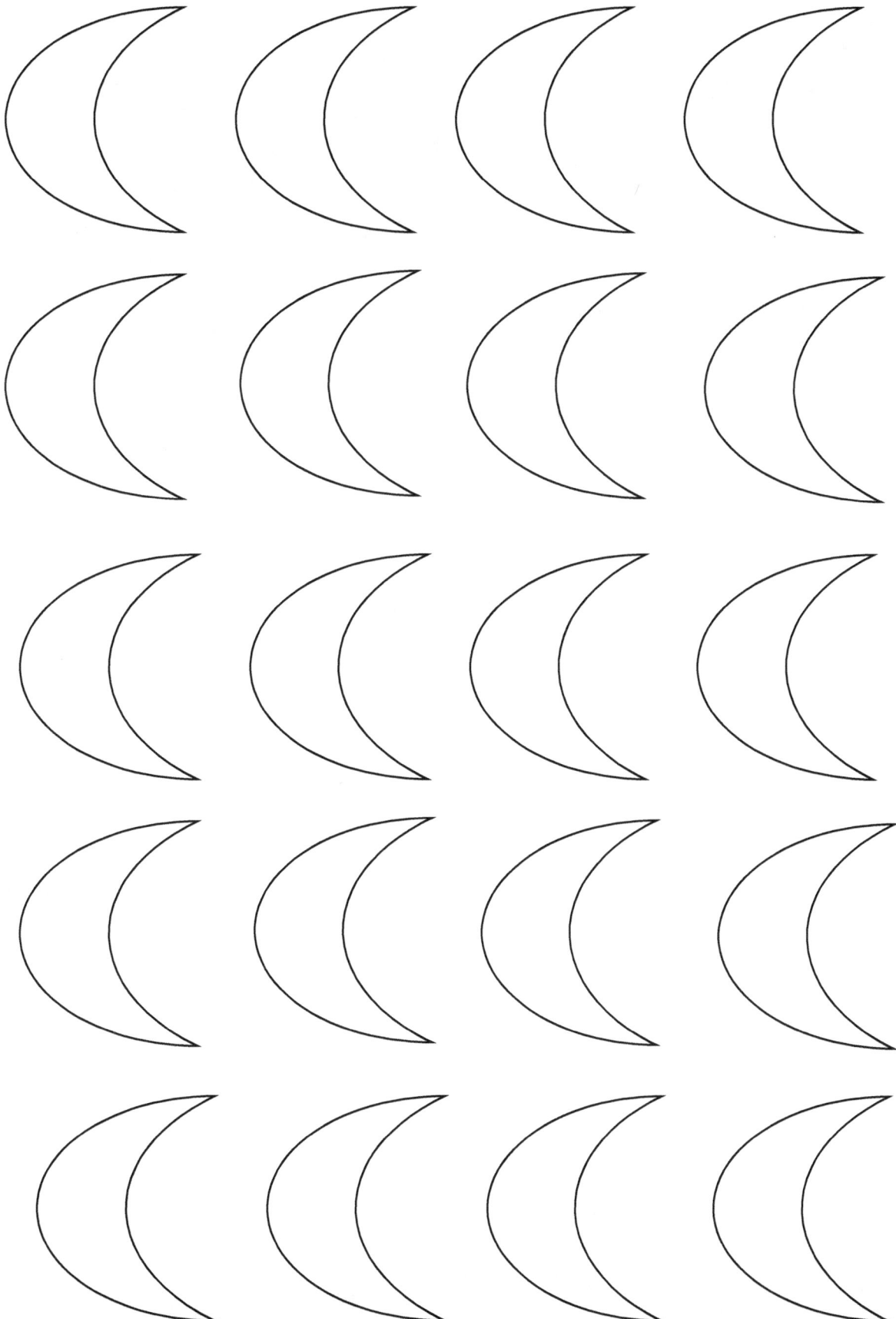

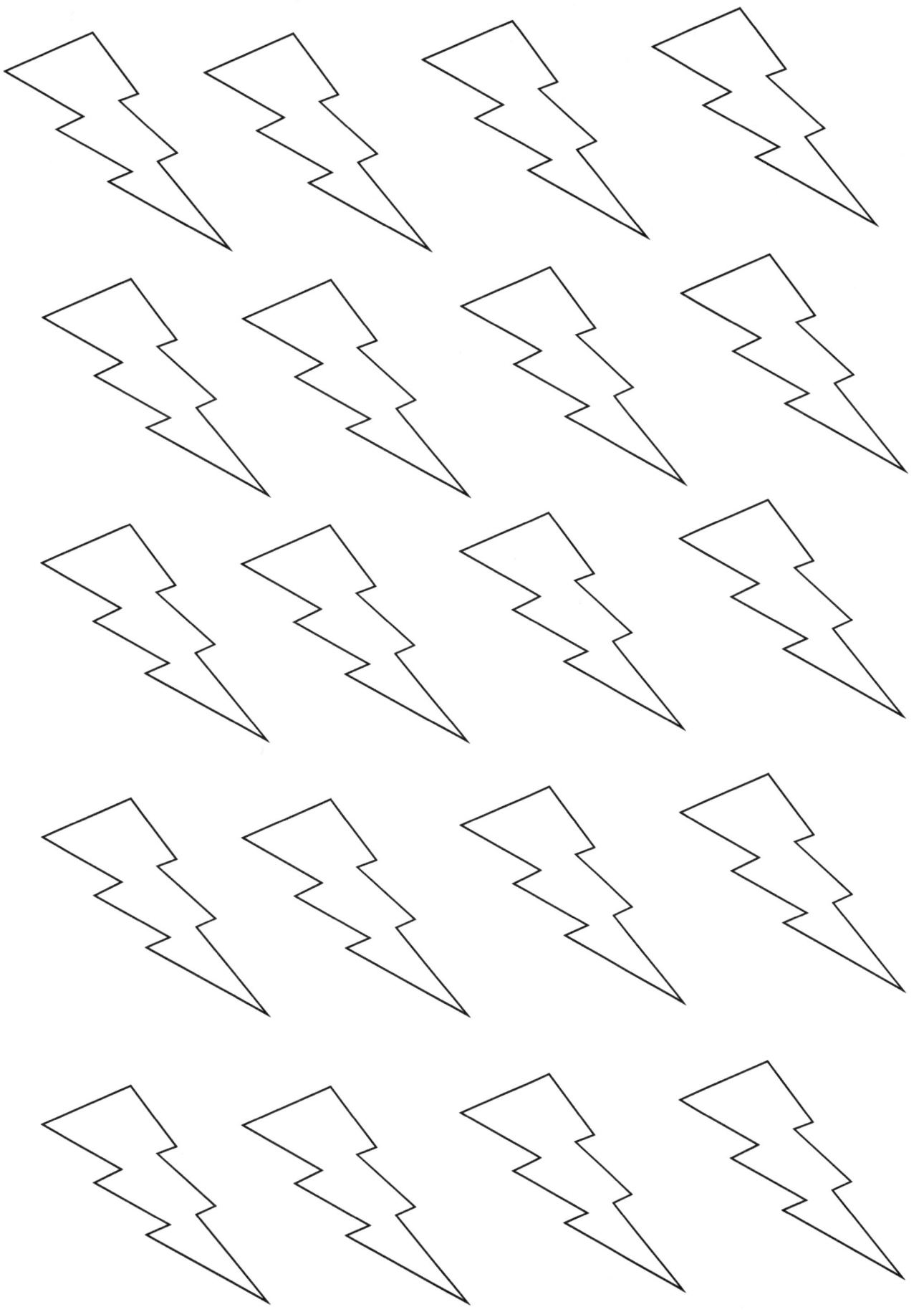

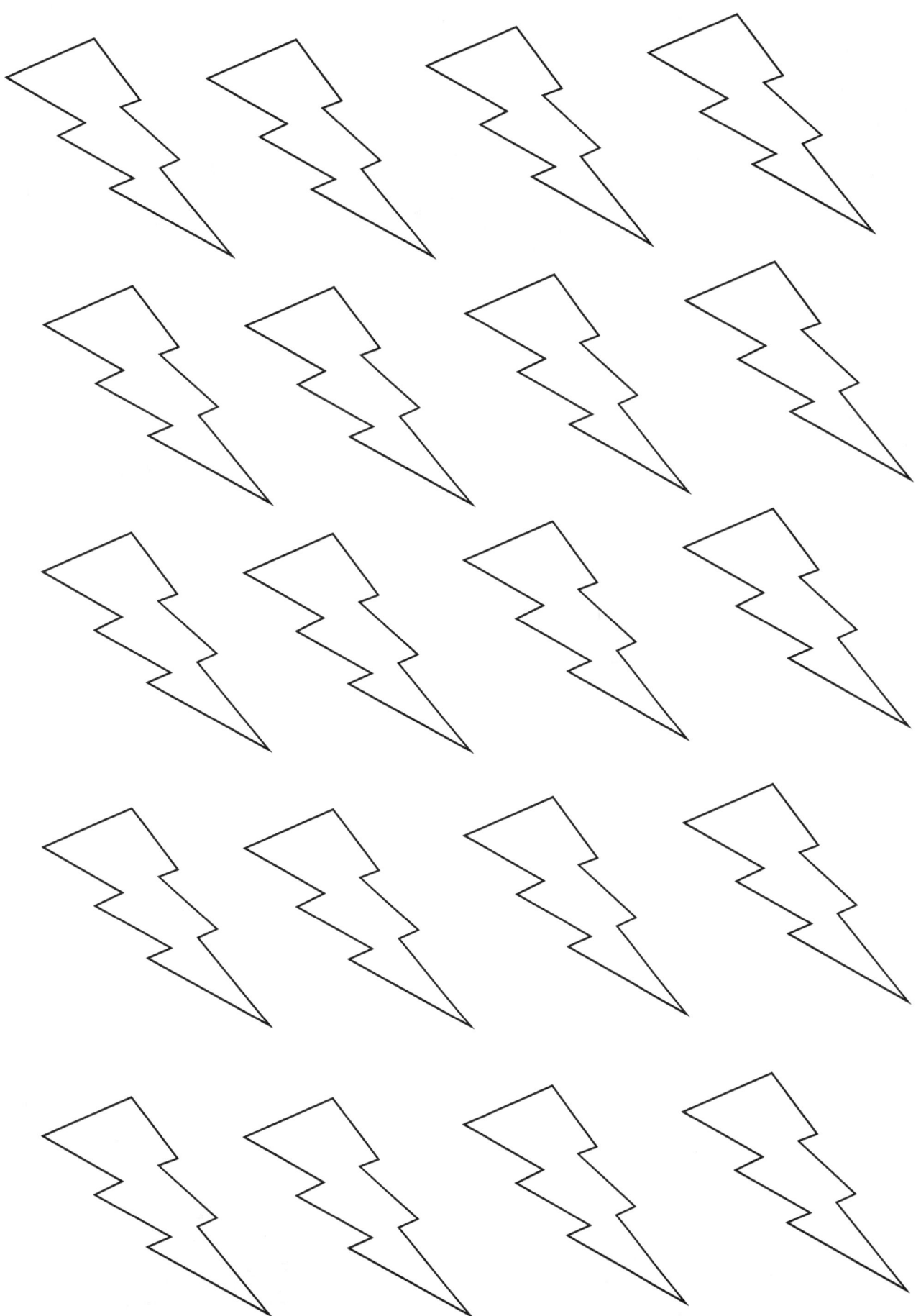

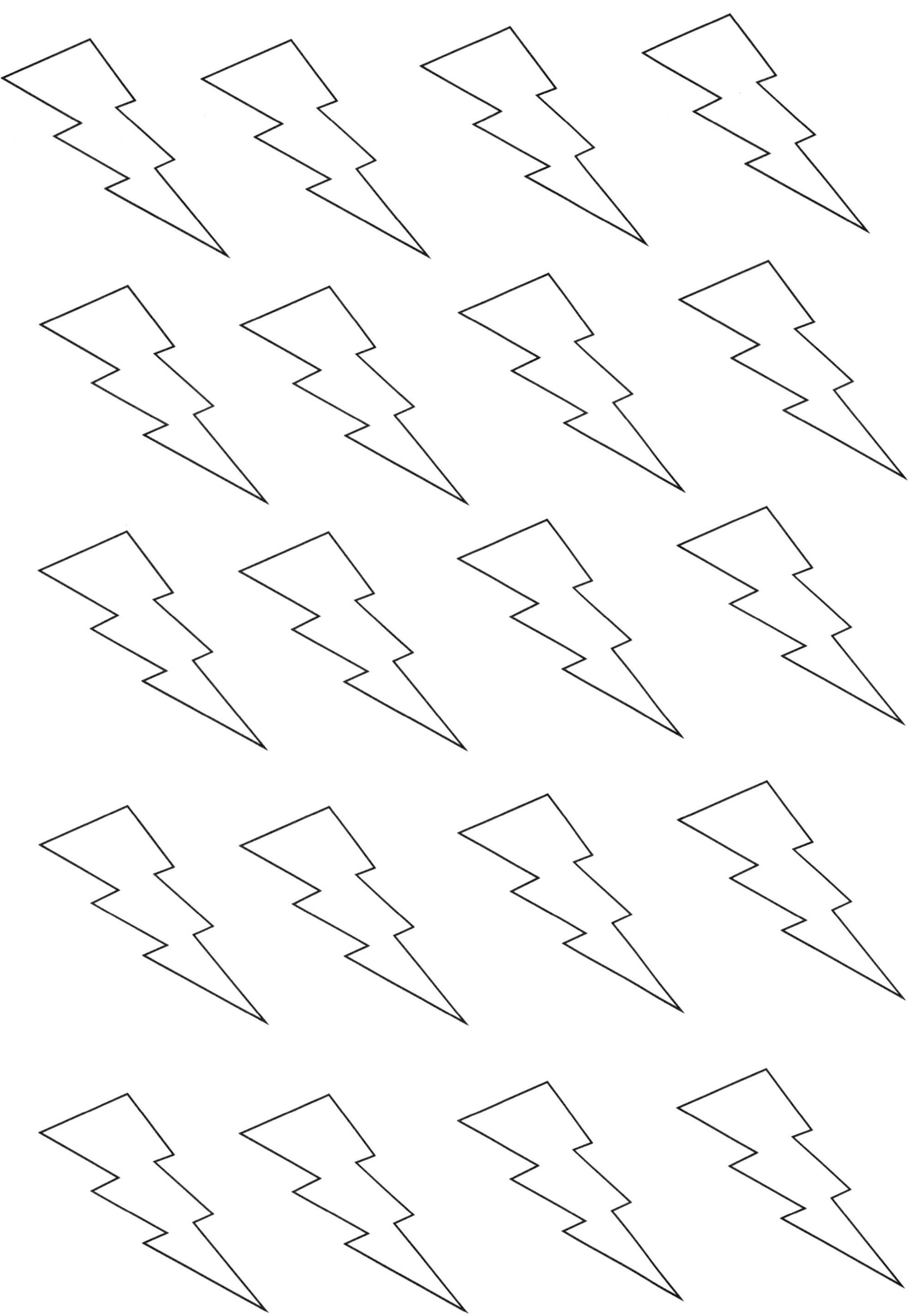

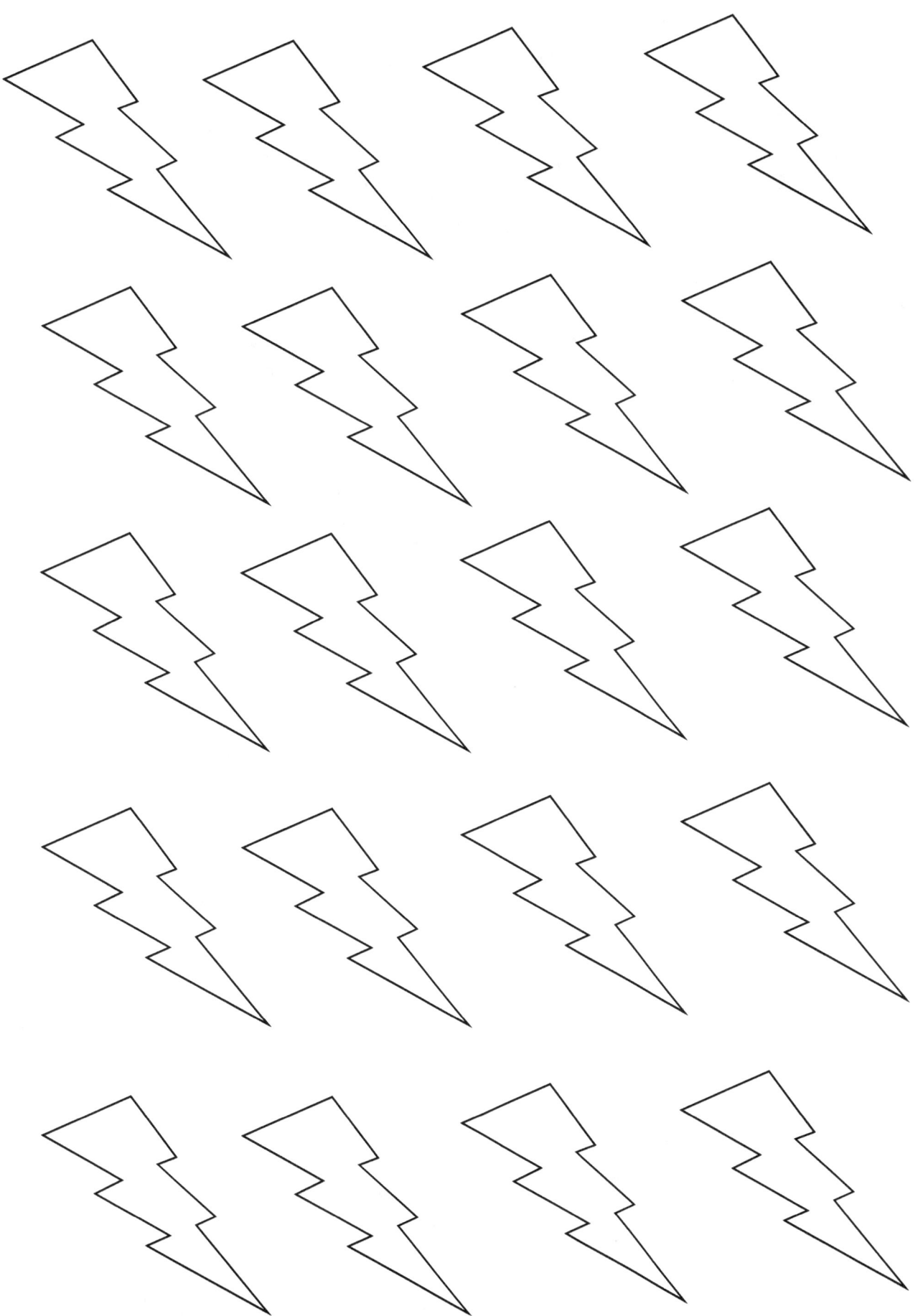

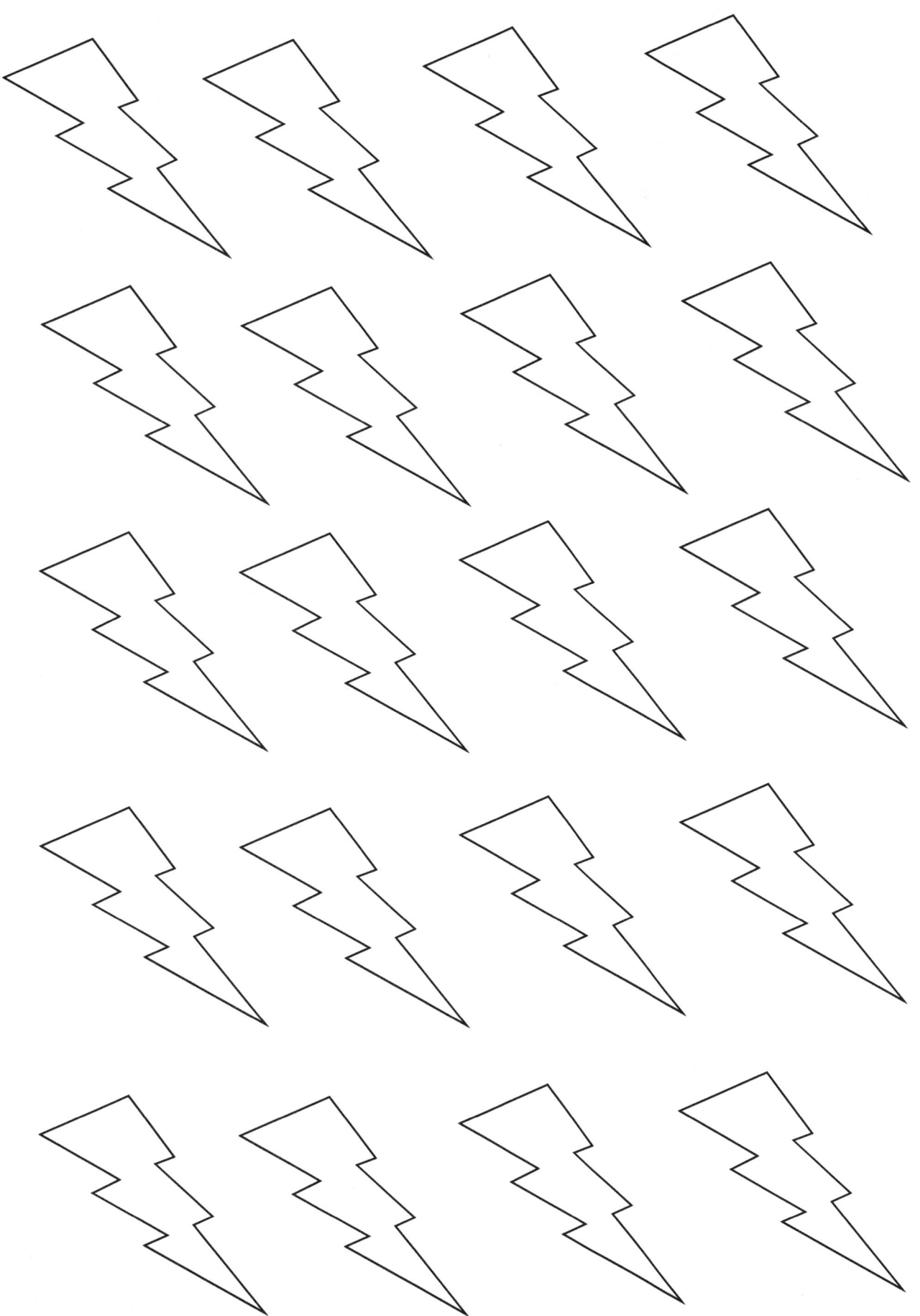

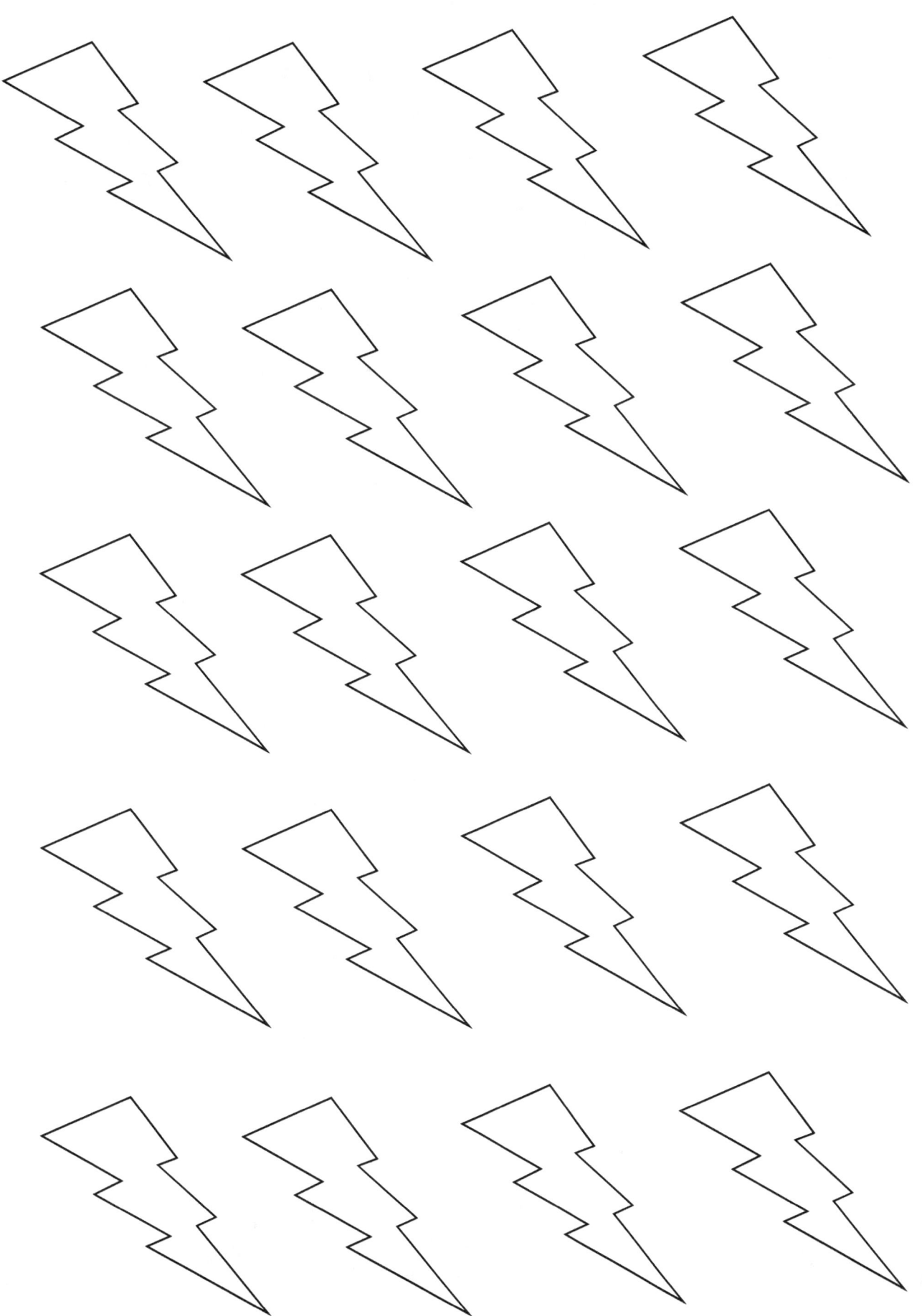

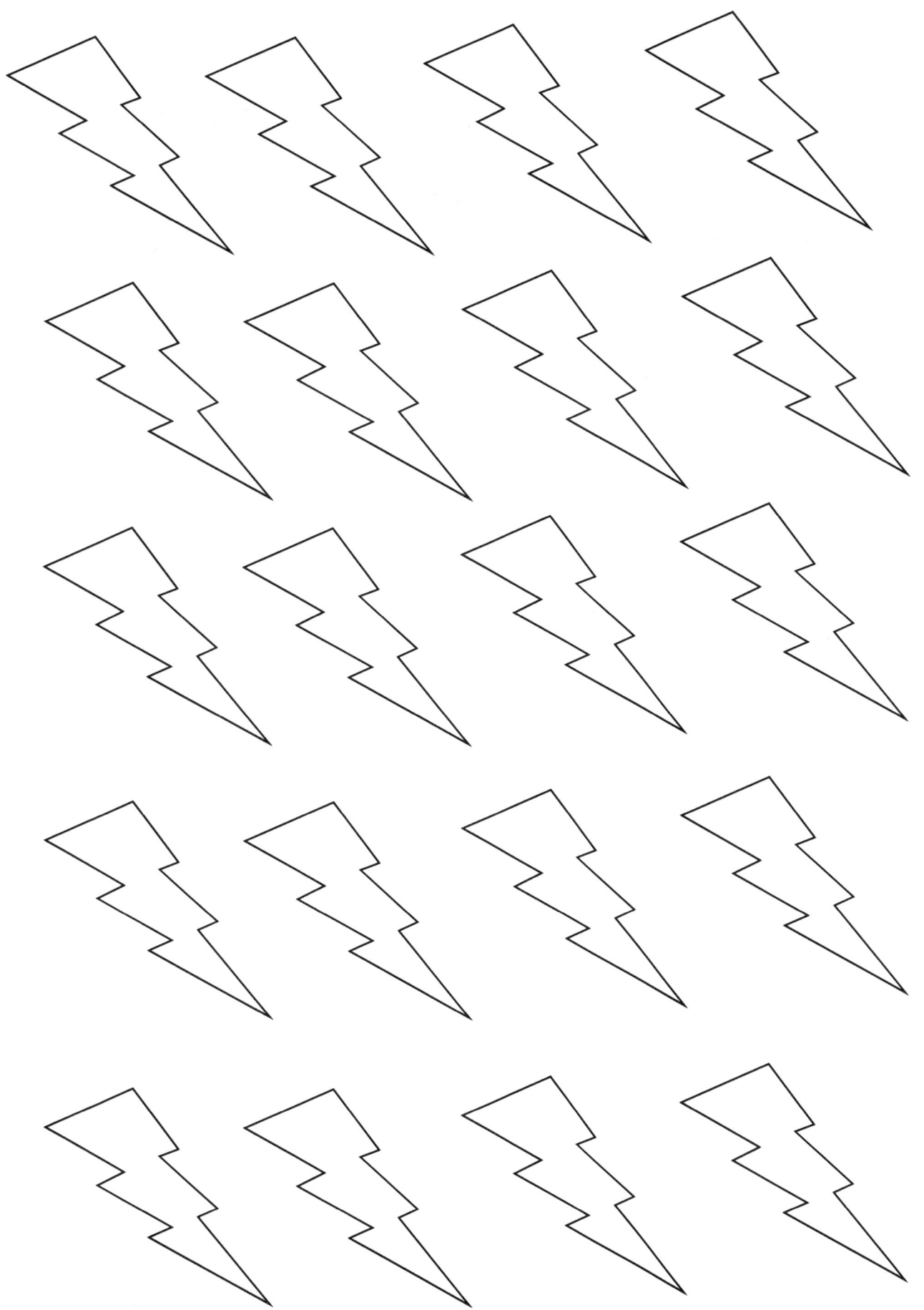

Notes and thoughts on brands and types of art supplies

Supplies I need to reorder:

_____
_____
_____
_____
_____
_____
_____
_____
_____
_____
_____
_____
_____
_____
_____
_____
_____
_____
_____
_____
_____
_____
_____
_____
_____
_____
_____
_____